I0167729

Tennessee Bingo Book

COMPLETE BINGO GAME IN A BOOK

Written By Rebecca Stark

ISBN 978-0-87386-535-7

Educational Books 'n' Bingo

Printed in the U.S.A.

DIRECTIONS

INCLUDED:

List of Terms

Templates for Additional Terms and Clues

2 Clues per Term

30 Unique Bingo Cards

Markers

1. **Either cut apart the book or make copies of ALL the sheets. You might want to make an extra copy of the clue sheets to use for introduction and review. Keep the sheets in an envelope for easy reuse.**

2. Cut apart the call cards with terms and clues.

3. Pass out one bingo card per student. There are enough for a class of 30.

4. Pass out markers. You may cut apart the markers included in this book or use any other small items of your choice.

5. Decide whether or not you will require the entire card to be filled. Requiring the entire card to be filled provides a better review. However, if you have a short time to fill, you may prefer to have them do the just the border or some other format. Tell the class before you begin what is required.

6. There are 50 terms. Read the list before you begin. If there are any terms that have not been covered in class, you may want to read to the students the term and clues before you begin.

7. There is a blank space in the middle of each card. You can instruct the students to use it as a free space or you can write in answers to cover terms not included. Of course, in this case you would create your own clues. (Templates provided.)

8. Shuffle the cards and place them in a pile. Two or three clues are provided for each term. If you plan to play the game with the same group more than once, you might want to choose a different clue for each game. If not, you may choose to use more than one clue.

9. Be sure to keep the cards you have used for the present game in a separate pile. When a student calls, "Bingo," he or she will have to verify that the correct answers are on his or her card AND that the markers were placed in response to the proper questions. Pull out the cards that are on the student's card keeping them in the order they were used in the game. Read each clue as it was given and ask the student to identify the correct answer from his or her card.

10. If the student has the correct answers on the card AND has shown that they were marked in response to the *correct questions,* then that student is the winner and the game is over. If the student does not have the correct answers on the card OR he or she marked the answers in response to *the wrong questions,* then the game continues until there is a proper winner.

11. If you want to play again, reshuffle the cards and begin again.

Have fun!

TERMS INCLUDED

Alluvial Plain

Aviation Hall of Fame

Blue Ridge

Border(s)

Chattanooga

Cherokee

Civil War

Climate

Clingmans Dome

Confederate States of America

County (-ies)

David (Davy) Crockett

Crop(s)

Cumberland Plateau

Executive Branch

Flag

Flower

Grand Ole Opry

Great Smokies

Highland Rim

Industry (-ies)

Inner Coastal Plain

Insect(s)

Andrew Jackson

Andrew Johnson

Judicial Branch

Knoxville

Legislative Branch

Limestone

Livestock

Memphis

Mined

Mockingbird(s)

Motto

Murfreesboro

Nashville

Nashville Basin

Native American

Pearl(s)

James K. Polk

Elvis Presley

Raccoon(s)

Seal

Song(s)

Tree(s)

Turtle

Union

Valley and Ridge

Volunteer State

Walking Horse(s)

Additional Terms

Choose as many additional terms as you would like and write them in the squares. Repeat each as desired.
Cut out the squares and randomly distribute them to the class.
Instruct the students to place their square on the center space of their card.

Tennessee Bingo

Clues for
Additional Terms

Write two clues for each of your additional terms.

1.

2.

1.

2.

1.

2.

1.

2.

.

1.

2.

1.

2.

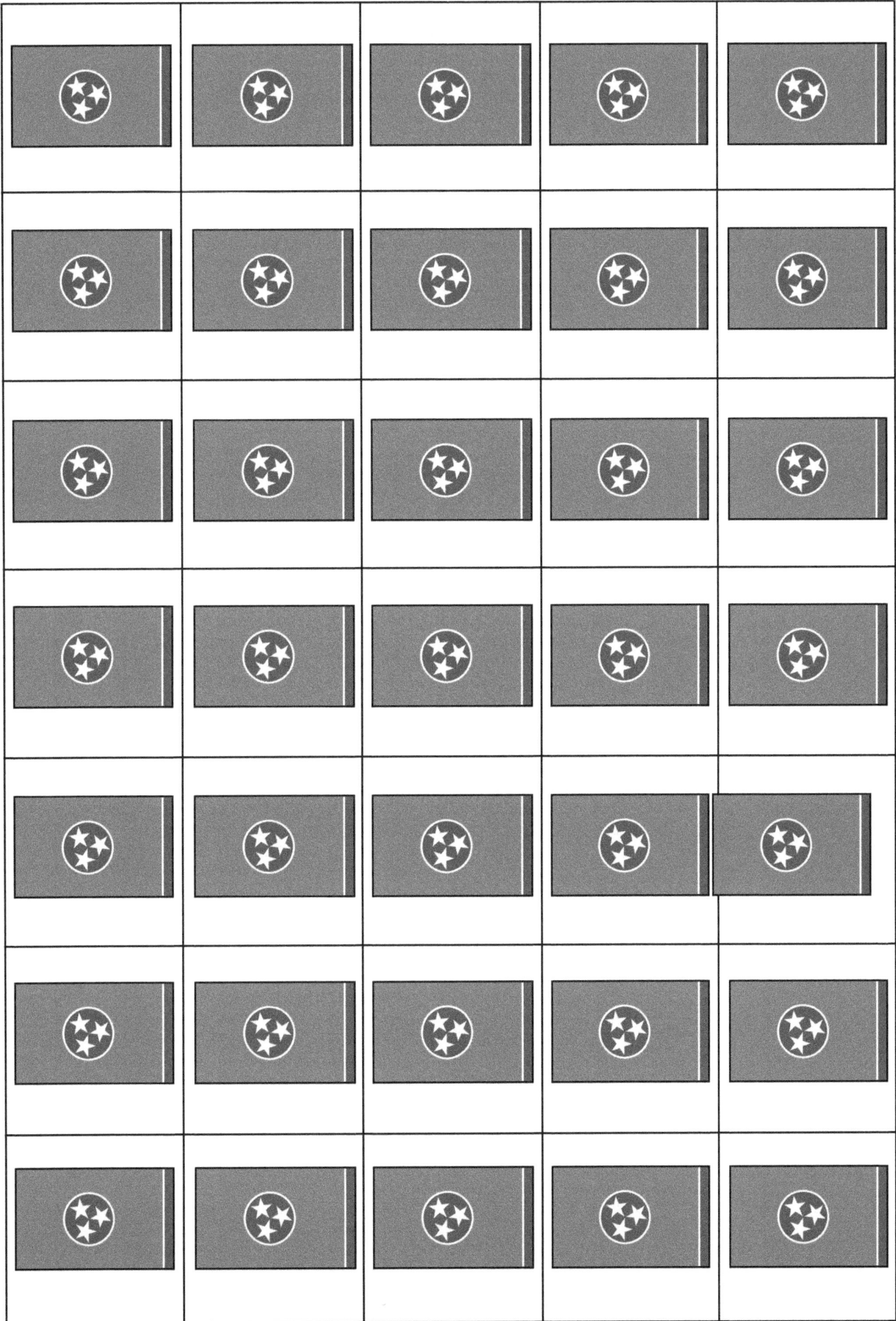

Alluvial Plain 1. The Mississippi ___ is situated along the State's western border. 2. The western boundary of this flood plain is the Mississippi River. East of the ___ is an area of high ground called the Chickasaw Bluffs.	**Aviation Hall of Fame** 1. The Tennessee ___ is located at the Gatlingburg-Pigeon Forge Airport in Sevier County. 2. The Tennessee ___ was honors aviation pioneers and leaders.
Blue Ridge 1. The ___ Region, or Unaka Mountain Region, along the eastern border of the state has the highest and most rugged terrain in the state. 2. The ___ Region is part of the Appalachian Mountains. It includes the Great Smoky Mountains, the Chilhowee Mountains, and the Snowbird Mountains.	**Border(s)** 1. Tennessee and Missouri each share ___ with eight states. That is more than any other state. 2. The states that ___ Tennessee are Kentucky, Virginia, North Carolina, Georgia, Alabama, Mississippi, Missouri, and Arkansas.
Chattanooga 1. ___ is nicknamed "Scenic City." It is well known because of the 1941 hit song "___ Choo Choo," composed by Glenn Miller and his orchestra. 2. The Tennessee Valley Railroad Museum is located in ___.	**Cherokee** 1. Sequoyah created a syllabary that made reading and writing in ___ possible. 2. The word "Tennessee" comes from *Tanasi,* a major ___ town in what is now southeastern Tennessee.
Civil War 1. Only Virginia saw more ___battles than Tennessee. 2. Although Tennessee became a part of the Confederacy, in many areas strong pro-Union sentiments remained.	**Climate** 1. In general, Tennessee has a temperate ___, with warm summers and mild winters. 2. The ___ in Tennessee varies because of the variation in topography.
Clingmans Dome 1. At 6,643 feet, ___ is the highest point in the state. 2. ___ is in the Great Smoky Mountains in the Blue Ridge Region. Tennessee Bingo	**Confederate States of America** 1. Tennessee was the last to secede and join the ___. 2. The President of the ___ was Jefferson Davis. © Barbara M. Peller

County (-ies) 1. Tennessee has 95 ___. 2. Shelby is the largest ___ in both area and population.	**David (Davy) Crockett** 1. This frontiersman, soldier, and politician was born near Limestone, Tennessee, in 1786. 2. This legendary frontiersman died at the Battle of the Alamo in San Antonio in 1836.
Crop(s) 1. Soybeans, greenhouse and nursery products, cotton, corn for grain, and tobacco are the important field ___. 2. Soybeans are the most important field ___.	**Cumberland Plateau** 1. The ___ is west of the Ridge and Valley and east of the Highland Rim regions. 2. The ___ is part of the Appalachian Plateau. The topography varies, and in some places the surface has been cut by stream valleys and gorges.
Executive Branch 1. The ___ of government enforces the laws and runs the day-to-day operations of the state. The governor is head of this branch. 2. The governor, the lieutenant governor, the attorney general, the secretary of state, the treasurer, and the comptroller are all part of the ___ of government. The present-day governor is [fill in].	**Flag** 1. The 3 white stars on the state ___ represent Eastern Tennessee, Middle Tennessee, and Western Tennessee. 2. The large field on the state ___ is crimson red. A circular field of blue surrounds the 3 stars.
Flower 1. The state cultivated ___ is the iris. 2. The state wild___ is the passion ___.	**Grand Ole Opry** 1. The ___ is a weekly stage show and radio broadcast featuring American country music. 2. This country-music stage concert has been broadcast on WSM since October 1925.
Great Smokies 1. The ___ are in the Blue Ridge Region. They are part of an International biosphere reserve* and have been designated a UNESCO World Heritage Site. 2. The name comes from the natural fog that often hangs over the range. *A biosphere reserve is an environmentally sensitive area with protected status to preserve natural ecological conditions. Tennessee Bingo	**Highland Rim** 1. The ___ region is between the Inner Coastal Plain and the Cumberland Plateau. The north is sometimes called the Pennyroyal Region. 2. The ___ is the largest geographic region. This elevated plain surrounds the Nashville Basin, dividing the region into the Western ___ and the Eastern ___.

Industry (-ies) 1. Mining, food processing, electric power, music, transportation equipment, farming, and tourism are important ___. 2. Processed foods, such as grain products, bread, breakfast cereals, and flour, are an important sector of the manufacturing ___.	**Inner Coastal Plain** 1. The ___ is part of the larger Gulf Coastal Plain. It lies west of the Highland Rim. 2. The ___ is divided into three sections. From west to east, the sections are the Mississippi Alluvial Plain; the relatively flat West Tennessee Plain, or Tennessee Bottoms; and the hilly West Tennessee Uplands.
Insect(s) 1. Several ___ are official state symbols. They include the honeybee, the firefly, the ladybug, and the zebra swallowtail. 2. The honeybee is the state agricultural ___. It is an official symbol in 17 states, probably because it is so important to agriculture.	**Andrew Jackson** 1. ___ was the seventh President of the United States. 2. The Hermitage, the home of President ___, is in Nashville.
Andrew Johnson 1. ___ became the 17th President when President Lincoln was assassinated. 2. President Lincoln appointed ___ military governor of Tennessee during the Civil War. He later became Lincoln's Vice President.	**Judicial Branch** 1. The judicial branch of government interprets the laws and runs the courts. 2. The Supreme Court is the highest court in the ___ of Tennessee government.
Knoxville 1. ___ is the third largest city in Tennessee after Memphis and Nashville. 2. The flagship campus of the University of Tennessee is located in ___.	**Legislative Branch** 1. The ___ of Tennessee government makes the laws. 2. The ___ of Tennessee government consists of the House and Senate.
Limestone 1. ___ is the state rock. 2. ___ is a sedimentary rock. Tennessee marble, the metamorphic form of ___, is widely used in public and private buildings.	**Livestock** 1. Beef cattle, broilers, dairy products, hogs, and chicken eggs are important ___ products. 2. The most valuable ___ products are beef cattle and broilers, or young chickens.

Tennessee Bingo

Memphis 1. ___ is the largest city in Tennessee. 2. ___ is called the "Birthplace of the Blues."	**Mined** 1. Construction materials, zinc, coal, oil, and natural gas are important ___ products. 2. Construction materials ___ or quarried in the state include sandstone, marble, crushed stone, limestone, clay, sand, and gravel.
Mockingbird(s) 1. The ___ is the state bird. 2. ___can sing up to 200 songs; they often copy the songs and sounds of other creatures.	**Motto** 1. "Agriculture and Commerce" is the state ___. 2. The ___ is on Tennessee's Great Seal.
Murfreesboro 1. The Battle of Stones River, or the Second Battle of ___, was one of the bloodiest conflicts of the Civil War. 2. This growing city is home to Middle Tennessee State University.	**Nashville** 1. ___ is the state capital. 2. The Grand Ole Opry and the Country Music Hall of Fame and Museum are in this city.
Nashville Basin 1. This pear-shaped area in the center of the state is surrounded by the Highland Rim. 2. The ___ is also called the Central Basin. This densely populated area is characterized by rich, fertile farms. Nashville is in the northwestern part.	**Native American** 1. ___ tribes indigenous to Tennessee include the Cherokee, the Chickasaw, the Koasati, the Quapaw, the Shawnee, and the Yuchi. 2. ___ tribes were forced to relocate following the Indian Removal Act of 1830. The Cherokee called their forced relocation the "Trail of Tears."
Pearl(s) 1. The Tennessee River ___ is the official state gem. 2. The Tennessee River ___ Farm is located at the Birdsong Resort and Marina, near Camden. The ___ are cultivated in mussels.	**James K. Polk** 1. ___ was governor of Tennessee and the 11th President of the United States. 2. The home in which ___ resided from 1818 to 1824 is in Columbia. It is a Federal-style brick house built in 1816.

Tennessee Bingo

Elvis Presley 1. Graceland Mansion in Memphis was the home of ___. 2. ___ moved to Memphis with his family at the age of 13.	**Raccoon(s)** 1. This mammal is the official state wild animal. 2. ___ were hunted for their water-repellent fur. So many were killed that a tax was imposed to prevent their extinction in the 1800s.
Seal 1. The design of the Great ___ contains an image of a plow, a sheaf of wheat, and a cotton plant. 2. The Roman numerals on the state's Great ___ represent Tennessee as the 16th state.	**Song(s)** 1. Music is very important to the state. This is shown by its 11 official state ___! 2. "My Tennessee," by Frances Hannah Tranum, is the official public school ___.
Tree(s) 1. The state has 2 official ___: the tulip poplar and the Eastern red cedar. 2. The tulip poplar was chosen as the state ___ because it was used by pioneers to build houses and farm buildings.	**Turtle** 1. The state reptile is the Eastern box ___. 2. The Eastern box ___ has a lifespan from 30 to 60 years. it grows to about 6 inches in length.
Union 1. Tennessee joined the ___ on June 1, 1796. 2. When Tennessee joined the ___, it became the 16th state.	**Valley and Ridge** 1. The ___ Region is between the Cumberland Plateau and the Blue Ridge regions. 2. The ___ Region is covered by fertile valleys separated by wooded ridges. The western section is called The Great Valley. The ridges and valleys in the north generally have higher elevations.
Volunteer State 1. The nickname of Tennessee is the ___. 2. This nickname was earned during the War of 1812, when thousands of Tennesseans enlisted in response to Governor Blount's call for volunteers.	**Walking Horse(s)** 1. The Tennessee ___ is the state horse. 2. Tennessee ___ were developed by farmers in the Tennessee bluegrass region combining the genes of thoroughbreds and other breeds.
Tennessee Bingo	© Barbara M. Peller

Tennessee Bingo

Native American	Limestone	Aviation Hall of Fame	Great Smokies	Border(s)
Flag	Alluvial Plain	Union	Livestock	Elvis Presley
Turtle	Legislative Branch		Murfreesboro	Valley and Ridge
Tree(s)	James K. Polk	Song(s)	Knoxville	Mined
Motto	Inner Coastal Plain	Cumberland Plateau	Walking Horse(s)	Andrew Jackson

Tennessee Bingo

Tree(s)	Turtle	Flower	Pearl(s)	Judicial Branch
Mined	David (Davy) Crockett	Civil War	James K. Polk	Mockingbird(s)
Clingmans Dome	Inner Coastal Plain		Insect(s)	Song(s)
Nashville	Nashville Basin	Legislative Branch	Volunteer State	Border(s)
Elvis Presley	Union	Cumberland Plateau	Flag	Walking Horse(s)

Tennessee Bingo

Inner Coastal Plain	Song(s)	David (Davy) Crockett	Knoxville	Turtle
Mined	Alluvial Plain	Climate	Limestone	Industry (-ies)
James K. Polk	Union		Mockingbird(s)	Blue Ridge
Legislative Branch	Clingmans Dome	Motto	Nashville	Flower
Walking Horse(s)	Confederate States of America	Cumberland Plateau	Volunteer State	Judicial Branch

Tennessee Bingo: Card No. 3

© Barbara M. Peller

Tennessee Bingo

Legislative Branch	Mockingbird(s)	Aviation Hall of Fame	Confederate States of America	Judicial Branch
Memphis	Cherokee	Limestone	Pearl(s)	Turtle
Murfreesboro	Nashville		Andrew Jackson	Great Smokies
Song(s)	Alluvial Plain	Union	Cumberland Plateau	Civil War
County (-ies)	Elvis Presley	Chattanooga	Walking Horse(s)	Valley and Ridge

Tennessee Bingo: Card No. 4

Tennessee Bingo

Elvis Presley	Border(s)	James K. Polk	Civil War	Confederate States of America
Memphis	Song(s)	Climate	Insect(s)	Alluvial Plain
Aviation Hall of Fame	Valley and Ridge		Livestock	Highland Rim
Andrew Jackson	Judicial Branch	Native American	Volunteer State	Crop(s)
David (Davy) Crockett	Cumberland Plateau	Turtle	Legislative Branch	Murfreesboro

Tennessee Bingo

Blue Ridge	Mockingbird(s)	Flower	Judicial Branch	Valley and Ridge
Knoxville	James K. Polk	Crop(s)	Limestone	Turtle
Pearl(s)	County (-ies)		Cherokee	Insect(s)
Cumberland Plateau	Motto	Volunteer State	Chattanooga	Aviation Hall of Fame
Mined	Civil War	Native American	Murfreesboro	Executive Branch

Tennessee Bingo: Card No. 6

Tennessee Bingo

Native American	Mockingbird(s)	Highland Rim	Song(s)	David (Davy) Crockett
Mined	Judicial Branch	Inner Coastal Plain	Alluvial Plain	Memphis
Valley and Ridge	Great Smokies		Insect(s)	Cherokee
Legislative Branch	Nashville	Climate	Tree(s)	Clingmans Dome
Cumberland Plateau	Confederate States of America	Volunteer State	Chattanooga	Blue Ridge

Tennessee Bingo: Card No. 7

Tennessee Bingo

Murfreesboro	Mockingbird(s)	Grand Ole Opry	Knoxville	Cherokee
Memphis	Aviation Hall of Fame	Pearl(s)	Valley and Ridge	Civil War
Executive Branch	Confederate States of America		Judicial Branch	Border(s)
Walking Horse(s)	Legislative Branch	Tree(s)	County (-ies)	Nashville
Union	Cumberland Plateau	Chattanooga	James K. Polk	Mined

Tennessee Bingo

Insect(s)	David (Davy) Crockett	Inner Coastal Plain	Executive Branch	Confederate States of America
County (-ies)	Judicial Branch	Murfreesboro	James K. Polk	Mockingbird(s)
Industry (-ies)	Native American		Alluvial Plain	Grand Ole Opry
Crop(s)	Border(s)	Motto	Livestock	Highland Rim
Nashville	Volunteer State	Climate	Tree(s)	Andrew Jackson

Tennessee Bingo

Tree(s)	Knoxville	Cherokee	Pearl(s)	Executive Branch
Valley and Ridge	Civil War	Limestone	Alluvial Plain	Judicial Branch
Confederate States of America	Mockingbird(s)		Great Smokies	Clingmans Dome
Motto	Andrew Jackson	Crop(s)	Volunteer State	Industry (-ies)
Climate	Mined	Flower	Elvis Presley	Murfreesboro

Tennessee Bingo: Card No. 10

© Barbara M. Peller

Tennessee Bingo

Blue Ridge	Mockingbird(s)	James K. Polk	Crop(s)	Mined
Grand Ole Opry	Industry (-ies)	Livestock	Insect(s)	Limestone
Memphis	Judicial Branch		Flower	Inner Coastal Plain
Climate	Turtle	Volunteer State	Confederate States of America	Tree(s)
County (-ies)	Cumberland Plateau	Native American	Chattanooga	David (Davy) Crockett

Tennessee Bingo: Card No. 11

Tennessee Bingo

David (Davy) Crockett	Border(s)	Industry (-ies)	Knoxville	Insect(s)
Inner Coastal Plain	Mined	Aviation Hall of Fame	Chattanooga	Alluvial Plain
Native American	Highland Rim		Valley and Ridge	Pearl(s)
Cumberland Plateau	Nashville	Judicial Branch	Tree(s)	Memphis
Mockingbird(s)	Grand Ole Opry	Confederate States of America	County (-ies)	Civil War

Tennessee Bingo

Crop(s)	Border(s)	Blue Ridge	Industry (-ies)	Valley and Ridge
Aviation Hall of Fame	Grand Ole Opry	Judicial Branch	Insect(s)	Clingmans Dome
Knoxville	Civil War		Inner Coastal Plain	Highland Rim
Murfreesboro	Volunteer State	Cherokee	Confederate States of America	Tree(s)
Cumberland Plateau	Andrew Jackson	Chattanooga	Native American	Livestock

Tennessee Bingo: Card No. 13

Tennessee Bingo

Flag	Judicial Branch	James K. Polk	Insect(s)	County (-ies)
Civil War	Native American	Industry (-ies)	Alluvial Plain	Mockingbird(s)
Crop(s)	Great Smokies		Flower	Climate
Andrew Jackson	Volunteer State	Confederate States of America	Cherokee	Blue Ridge
Cumberland Plateau	Pearl(s)	Clingmans Dome	Mined	Murfreesboro

Tennessee Bingo

Livestock	Insect(s)	James K. Polk	David (Davy) Crockett	Knoxville
Blue Ridge	Flower	Limestone	Aviation Hall of Fame	County (-ies)
Valley and Ridge	Native American		Turtle	Mockingbird(s)
Cumberland Plateau	Industry (-ies)	Grand Ole Opry	Volunteer State	Crop(s)
Mined	Nashville	Chattanooga	Executive Branch	Inner Coastal Plain

Tennessee Bingo: Card No. 15

Tennessee Bingo

Cherokee	Industry (-ies)	Grand Ole Opry	Executive Branch	Nashville Basin
Pearl(s)	Clingmans Dome	Highland Rim	Memphis	Great Smokies
Crop(s)	Border(s)		Valley and Ridge	Inner Coastal Plain
Legislative Branch	Civil War	Cumberland Plateau	Livestock	Tree(s)
County (-ies)	Seal	Chattanooga	Nashville	Mockingbird(s)

Tennessee Bingo

Climate	Raccoon(s)	Andrew Johnson	Industry (-ies)	Flag
Livestock	County (-ies)	Volunteer State	Great Smokies	Highland Rim
Insect(s)	Murfreesboro		Seal	Grand Ole Opry
Andrew Jackson	Mined	Tree(s)	James K. Polk	Clingmans Dome
Motto	Crop(s)	David (Davy) Crockett	Knoxville	Border(s)

Tennessee Bingo: Card No. 17

© Barbara M. Peller

Tennessee Bingo

Executive Branch	Confederate States of America	Civil War	Crop(s)	Pearl(s)
Mockingbird(s)	Climate	Motto	Valley and Ridge	County (-ies)
Insect(s)	Clingmans Dome		Andrew Johnson	Aviation Hall of Fame
Border(s)	Limestone	Volunteer State	Tree(s)	Flower
Seal	Industry (-ies)	James K. Polk	Raccoon(s)	Blue Ridge

Tennessee Bingo

Valley and Ridge	Blue Ridge	Industry (-ies)	Grand Ole Opry	Tree(s)
Livestock	Knoxville	Mockingbird(s)	David (Davy) Crockett	Great Smokies
Raccoon(s)	Confederate States of America		Alluvial Plain	Turtle
Flower	Seal	Motto	Nashville	
Aviation Hall of Fame	Nashville Basin	Mined	Murfreesboro	Chattanooga

Tennessee Bingo

Flag	Raccoon(s)	Knoxville	Industry (-ies)	Chattanooga
Civil War	Inner Coastal Plain	Memphis	Motto	Pearl(s)
Border(s)	Highland Rim		Legislative Branch	Limestone
Elvis Presley	Union	Walking Horse(s)	Nashville	Seal
Song(s)	Murfreesboro	Nashville Basin	Tree(s)	Andrew Johnson

Tennessee Bingo

Livestock	Blue Ridge	Memphis	Industry (-ies)	Elvis Presley
Border(s)	Andrew Johnson	Cherokee	Grand Ole Opry	Native American
Clingmans Dome	Mined		Raccoon(s)	James K. Polk
Motto	David (Davy) Crockett	Seal	Andrew Jackson	Murfreesboro
Legislative Branch	Nashville Basin	Chattanooga	Climate	Nashville

Tennessee Bingo

Executive Branch	Flower	Andrew Johnson	Aviation Hall of Fame	Crop(s)
Pearl(s)	Knoxville	Turtle	Grand Ole Opry	Alluvial Plain
Civil War	Great Smokies		Native American	Highland Rim
Seal	Andrew Jackson	Nashville	Limestone	Memphis
Nashville Basin	Climate	Raccoon(s)	Clingmans Dome	Legislative Branch

Tennessee Bingo

Cherokee	Raccoon(s)	David (Davy) Crockett	Aviation Hall of Fame	Chattanooga
Blue Ridge	Flag	Mined	Livestock	Limestone
Flower	Crop(s)		Walking Horse(s)	Native American
Clingmans Dome	Nashville Basin	Seal	Climate	Nashville
Elvis Presley	Union	Murfreesboro	Motto	Andrew Johnson

Tennessee Bingo: Card No. 23

Tennessee Bingo

Cherokee	Murfreesboro	Flag	Raccoon(s)	Grand Ole Opry
Andrew Johnson	Chattanooga	Memphis	Pearl(s)	Native American
Highland Rim	Executive Branch		Crop(s)	Clingmans Dome
Elvis Presley	Walking Horse(s)	Seal	Climate	Border(s)
Song(s)	Legislative Branch	Nashville Basin	Knoxville	Union

Tennessee Bingo

Legislative Branch	Memphis	Raccoon(s)	James K. Polk	Andrew Johnson
Limestone	Border(s)	Livestock	Cherokee	Alluvial Plain
Andrew Jackson	Grand Ole Opry		Walking Horse(s)	Seal
Turtle	Elvis Presley	Union	Nashville Basin	Great Smokies
Chattanooga	Flag	Civil War	County (-ies)	Song(s)

Tennessee Bingo

Andrew Johnson	Raccoon(s)	Flower	Pearl(s)	Executive Branch
Motto	Knoxville	Grand Ole Opry	Flag	Cherokee
Andrew Jackson	Walking Horse(s)		Great Smokies	Legislative Branch
Climate	Aviation Hall of Fame	Elvis Presley	Nashville Basin	Seal
Highland Rim	County (-ies)	James K. Polk	Union	Song(s)

Tennessee Bingo

Flower	Civil War	Raccoon(s)	Flag	Inner Coastal Plain
Elvis Presley	Walking Horse(s)	Livestock	Seal	Alluvial Plain
Volunteer State	Union		Nashville Basin	Legislative Branch
Executive Branch	Blue Ridge	Memphis	Song(s)	Limestone
County (-ies)	Great Smokies	Andrew Johnson	Turtle	Highland Rim

Tennessee Bingo

Flower	Flag	Turtle	Raccoon(s)	Cherokee
Inner Coastal Plain	Andrew Johnson	Walking Horse(s)	Pearl(s)	Great Smokies
Union	Clingmans Dome		Highland Rim	Motto
Tree(s)	Executive Branch	Mined	Nashville Basin	Seal
Aviation Hall of Fame	Insect(s)	County (-ies)	Song(s)	Elvis Presley

Tennessee
Bingo

Andrew Johnson	Flag	Executive Branch	Livestock	Insect(s)
Nashville	Motto	Memphis	Highland Rim	Turtle
Andrew Jackson	Walking Horse(s)		Alluvial Plain	Raccoon(s)
Inner Coastal Plain	Elvis Presley	Judicial Branch	Nashville Basin	Seal
Cherokee	Grand Ole Opry	Song(s)	Blue Ridge	Union

Tennessee Bingo: Card No. 29

Tennessee Bingo

Confederate States of America	Raccoon(s)	Pearl(s)	Insect(s)	Seal
Limestone	Flag	Flower	Great Smokies	Alluvial Plain
Andrew Jackson	Crop(s)		Highland Rim	Memphis
Song(s)	Blue Ridge	Aviation Hall of Fame	Nashville Basin	Walking Horse(s)
Elvis Presley	Valley and Ridge	Union	Andrew Johnson	Turtle